Live, Retire, And Die

Curtis Newkirk

Dedication

To all those seeking financial
empowerment and wellness,
This book, "Money Matters: Your Guide to
Financial Wellness at Every Stage," is
dedicated to each individual on their
unique journey towards financial well-
being. In a world where the language of
money often seems complex and elusive,
this dedication serves as a reminder that
your pursuit of financial health is both
valid and significant.

To those who strive for stability and security, may this guide illuminate your path and provide the knowledge to make informed decisions at every turn. To the dreamers and visionaries, may these pages be a source of inspiration, offering insights that fuel your ambitions and transform them into tangible realities.

For those navigating through unexpected challenges, may the wisdom within these chapters serve as a compass, guiding you through the storms toward a place of financial resilience.

In recognition of the countless stories, aspirations, and aspirations woven into the fabric of our financial lives, this dedication is a tribute to the collective pursuit of financial well-being. May this book be a trusted companion on your journey, empowering you to navigate the twists and turns of money matters with confidence and clarity.
Here's to your financial wellness, at every stage.
With gratitude,
Curtis Newkirk

Chapter 1: "A Thanksgiving Tale" –
Page 7

Chapter 2: "The Starting Line:
Navigating Finances in Youth"- Page 9

Chapter 3: "Golden Years and Beyond:
Embracing Retirement and Legacy"-
Page 12

Chapter 4: " Navigating the Financial
Maze"- Page 14

Chapter 5: "Adulting & Money:
Mastering the Art of Financial
Independence"- Page 18

Chapter 6: "Beyond Budgets: Building
Wealth and Crafting Your Financial
Legacy"- Page 22

Chapter 1: "A Thanksgiving Tale"

Once upon a time, in the cozy town of Saraland, where the autumn breeze carried the scent of fallen leaves, a group of kids gathered at school. Thanksgiving break was over, and excitement filled the air. Among them was Oman, a 12-year-old with a smile that could light up the darkest room but a heart burdened with a silent struggle.

As the kids swapped stories about their family traditions for the upcoming Thanksgiving, Jake's silence didn't escape the notice of his friend Ethan. Concern etched Ethan's face as he approached Jake, gently asking what was on his mind. Jake hesitated but finally confided that his family was going through tough times, and this year's Thanksgiving feast would be a simple one – just chili dogs.

The news spread through the group, and a few snickers and judgmental glances followed. But then, a young man named Alex, who had overcome his fair share of hardships, stepped forward. With a genuine smile, he shared a story of his own Thanksgiving where hotdogs were the main course. His words created a moment of connection, breaking down judgment and fostering understanding.

Welcome to "Live, Retire, And Die." In this down-to-earth e- book, we'll take a journey through the various phases of life – from youth to retirement, and even beyond. Money is a constant companion on this journey, and understanding how to manage it effectively is crucial. Let's explore financial literacy in a human tone, making it relatable and accessible to everyone.

Chapter 2: "The Starting Line: Navigating Finances in Youth"

Alright, buckle up, because this chapter is your backstage pass to the wild rollercoaster ride called youth and finances. We've all been there – just out of college, wide-eyed, and ready to adult. But guess what? Adulting comes with a side of finances, and it's not as scary as it sounds. So, let's break it down.

The Budgeting Balancing Act:

Picture this: You land your first real job, and suddenly, there's money in your account. Hallelujah! But wait, where does it all go? That's where budgeting becomes your superhero. It's not about restricting yourself; it's about telling your money where to go instead of wondering where it went.

Create a budget that suits your style. Factor in the essentials like rent, utilities, groceries, and, of course, a little something for those weekend shenanigans. It's about finding the sweet spot between responsible adulting and keeping your sanity intact.

Student Loans: The Friendly Reminder: Now, let's address the elephant in the room — student loans. Those monthly reminders can be a bit of a buzzkill, right? But fear not, my friend. Understanding your interest rates, exploring repayment plans, and maybe even considering loan forgiveness programs can turn that student loan mountain into a manageable molehill.

Investing: It's Not Just for Wall Street Wizards:

Investing might sound like a word reserved for people in fancy suits yelling on trading floors, but it's not. It's for you, too. We're talking about dipping your toes into the stock market, maybe investing in a retirement account like a 401(k) or an IRA. The magic here? Compound interest. It's like a financial fairy godmother that makes your money grow over time. Let's make your money work for you, not the other way around.

Navigating Career Transitions:

As you move from part-time gigs to full-time adulting, there's a learning curve. Negotiating salaries, understanding benefits, and even managing workplace relationships – it's all part of the game. Remember, you're not alone in feeling a bit lost. Embrace the learning process and take notes along the way.

Balancing Act: Life, Fun, and Future:

Here's the secret sauce – finding the balance between living your best life now and setting the stage for an awesome future. It's not about living on ramen noodles to save every penny, but it's also not about blowing

your entire paycheck on the latest tech

gadget. It's about intentional choices that

align with your goals, both short-term and

long-term.

Facing the Unknown:

Life is full of surprises, and not all of them are pleasant. That's why having an emergency fund is like having a financial safety net. It's there for those unexpected curveballs that life loves to throw at you – a car breakdown, a sudden medical expense, or even a spontaneous road trip with friends. Be prepared for the unexpected, and your future self will thank you.

So, here's the deal: Youth is a time of exploration, discovery, and maybe a few financial fumbles. But that's okay. This chapter is your roadmap to navigate the exciting yet sometimes daunting starting line of financial adulthood. Budget like a boss, tackle those student loans with a game plan, dip your toes into investing waters, and remember – your financial journey is a marathon, not a sprint. Ready to take the first step? Let's dive in together.

Chapter 3: "Midlife Money Wisdom: Thriving in Adulthood"

Hey there, fellow adult in the wild jungle of responsibilities! Welcome to the chapter where we tackle the nitty-gritty of adulting and finance because let's face it – adulting comes with its fair share of challenges, bills, and a side order of wisdom. So, please grab a cup of coffee or your beverage, and let's dive into Midlife Money Wisdom.

Balancing Act: Dance of Finances and Responsibilities

Picture this: You've got a job that pays the bills, a family to look after, and a pet that insists on sitting on your laptop during Zoom meetings. The struggle is real, and so is the never-ending financial juggling act. Budgeting, my friend, is your trusty sidekick in this adventure.

In this section, we'll navigate the art of balancing finances and responsibilities without feeling like you're drowning in a sea of bills. We'll explore the intricacies of creating a family budget – one that keeps everyone fed, sheltered, and perhaps even entertained. From the mortgage to that unexpected plumbing issue, we've got your back in this adulting escapade.

Investing in the Future: Beyond the 401(k)

So, you're not just planning for your next vacation; you're thinking about that cozy retirement cottage with a view.

Welcome to the world of adulting! We'll demystify the jargon around 401(k)s, IRAs, and other investment options, making sure your future self gives you a high-five.

But hey, investing isn't just about the golden years; it's about the now too. We'll explore setting financial goals – be it the dream vacation, your kid's college fund, or that home office you've been eyeing. Get ready to make your money hustle for your dreams.

Emergency Fund: Your Financial Lifesaver

Life, the eternal game-changer, loves to throw curveballs. The car breaks down, your furry friend needs an unplanned visit to the vet, or your washing machine decides to go on strike. This is where the emergency fund struts onto the stage.

Building and maintaining an emergency fund is like giving yourself a superhero cape. We'll chat about the importance of having one, how to build it up, and why it's your financial safety net when life decides to throw a little chaos your way.

The Gentle Art of Saying No (Sometimes)

Adulting often involves perfecting the delicate dance of saying no – to that

Chapter 4: "Golden Years and Beyond: Embracing Retirement and Legacy"

Hey there, future retiree and legacy builder!

Welcome to the chapter where we're going

to chat about those golden years,

retirement plans, and the legacy you're

itching to leave behind.

Picture yourself on a porch swing with a cup

of coffee or tea – it's time to delve into the

world of "Golden Years and Beyond."

Transitioning to Relaxation Mode: Assessing Your Retirement Readiness

So, you've hit that stage where the daily

grind is starting to feel a bit too grindy. Retirement is calling, and it's time to assess whether you're ready to answer. In this section, we'll navigate the transition from the hustle and bustle of work life to the serene pace of retirement.

We'll talk about the financial side of things - assessing your retirement accounts, understanding your pension, and maybe even figuring out how Social Security fits into the picture. But it's not just about the numbers; it's about embracing a lifestyle that aligns with your dreams for the golden years.

Making Your Money Work for You: Smart Retirement Investing

Retirement doesn't mean bidding adieu to your finances; it's about making them work smarter, not harder. We'll explore the world of smart retirement investing – from optimizing your 401(k) to diversifying your portfolio. It's about ensuring your money is still growing while you're enjoying that well-deserved beach time or mastering the art of bird watching.

And let's not forget healthcare – a topic that becomes more critical as the candles on your birthday cake multiply. We'll discuss strategies for navigating healthcare expenses in retirement, from Medicare to long-term care planning. After all, staying healthy and financially secure go hand in hand in the golden years.

Crafting Your Legacy: Beyond Dollars and Cents

Now, let's talk about the legacy you want to leave behind. It's not just about the dollars and cents; it's about the impact you've made on the world. We'll explore the art of crafting your legacy, from passing on your values to your loved ones to making a difference in your community.

Estate planning, wills, and trusts – they might sound like topics reserved for legal dramas, but they're crucial aspects of ensuring your legacy is passed on smoothly. We'll guide you through the process with a mix of practical advice and a touch of empathy.

Facing the Inevitable: End-of-Life Planning

Okay, we're going to tackle a topic that's often whispered about but rarely discussed openly – end-of-life planning. It's not about being morbid; it's about facing the inevitable with grace and preparedness. From funeral costs to expressing your wishes through advanced directives, we'll navigate this conversation with the care it deserves.

Leaving a Financial Legacy: Beyond the Final Chapter

As we wind down this chapter, let's talk

about leaving a financial legacy. It's not just about what you leave behind for your loved ones; it's about the lessons they inherit. We'll explore strategies for passing on wealth responsibly and ensuring that your financial legacy aligns with your values.

Embracing the Later Stages with Financial Wisdom

As you stand at the threshold of the golden years and beyond, remember this – it's a phase to be embraced with financial wisdom and a sense of fulfillment. The transition to retirement, smart investing, legacy building, and end-of-life planning are all part of a

larger tapestry.

So, whether you're dreaming of a peaceful retirement on a beach, in the mountains, or simply in your backyard with a good book, know that your financial journey doesn't end here. It's a continuous adventure, and you hold the pen to your financial story.

In the golden years and beyond, it's about more than just money – it's about creating a legacy that extends beyond your lifetime. So, sit back, sip that coffee, and let's craft a financial future that not only supports your dreams but leaves a lasting impact on the world. Cheers to embracing the later stages with wisdom, joy, and a touch of financial flair!

Years later, the once group of kids had blossomed into a community of young adults, each on their unique journey. They had faced challenges and celebrated triumphs, but one common thread tied them together – the commitment to financial well-being.

As they reflected on their diverse paths, the realization dawned on them: financial literacy was not just a skill for the present; it was a tool that opened doors to a secure future. Gathered once more at the familiar park, their conversations had shifted from Thanksgiving menus to shared successes born from a challenging moment in their youth.

In a heartfelt conclusion, they

acknowledged that we all hold our future

in our hands, regardless of how life began.

It was a reminder that with knowledge,

determination, and support from one

another, anyone could navigate life's

financial challenges and shape a future

filled with prosperity and fulfillment.

So, as the sun set on Maplewood, the group

of friends looked ahead with confidence,

knowing that the lessons learned in the face

of adversity had paved the way for a future

they could shape and control.

Chapter 5: "Adulting & Money: Mastering the Art of Financial Independence"

Hey there, champions of adulthood! Welcome to the second chapter of your financial adventure – where we're kicking things up a notch and diving into the nitty-gritty of adulting with your finances. We get it; this chapter title sounds a bit official, but don't worry; we're still speaking your language.

Career Moves & Hustles:

Alright, let's talk about the big 'C' – Careers!

Your job is like the epicenter of your financial universe. We'll explore how to level up in your career game, from acing job interviews to negotiating that salary like a pro. Oh, and let's not forget the magic of side hustles – because who says you can't turn your passion project into some extra cash?

Life's a bit of a hustle, and we're here to guide you through the gig economy, freelance gigs, and all the creative ways you can stack those dollars while doing what you love. So, lace up those hustle boots; we're about to make your career journey a whole lot more exciting!

Tackling Taxes:

We get it – taxes aren't the most thrilling topic, but they're like the financial paperwork of adulthood. Don't worry; we've got your back. From deciphering W-4 forms to understanding deductions, we'll break down the tax game into digestible chunks. After all, a little tax knowledge can go a long way in keeping more of your hard-earned money in your pocket.

So, grab a cup of coffee (or your beverage of choice), and let's tackle taxes together. By the end of this section, you'll be ready to face tax season like a seasoned financial pro

– no stress, just savings.

Insurance 101:

Insurance might seem like a distant cousin of adulthood responsibilities, but it's your safety net against life's unexpected curveballs. We'll chat about the essentials – health insurance, car insurance, renter's insurance – and why they're not just financial necessities but your financial guardian angels.

Understanding insurance can be a game-changer in protecting your financial well-being, so let's debunk the myths, demystify the jargon, and make sure you're covered for whatever life throws your way. Because

adulting comes with a few bumps in the

road, and we want you to navigate them

with confidence.

Goals, Dreams, and the 'F' Word

(Retirement):

Alright, let's talk about the 'F' word – Retirement. It might seem like an eternity away, but trust us, future you will thank present you for thinking ahead. We'll dive into the magic of compound interest, the wonders of retirement accounts, and why starting early is like giving your future self a financial high-five.

It's not about sacrificing your present for an unknown future; it's about finding the balance between living your best life now and setting the stage for a comfortable, stress-free retirement later. So, let's make retirement planning a breeze and secure your financial future while enjoying the present.

Balancing Act – Life & Money:

Adulting is like walking a tightrope – a delicate balance between life and money. We'll chat about prioritizing financial goals, managing multiple responsibilities, and why self-care is not just a trendy buzzword but an essential part of your financial strategy.

Juggling work, personal life, and your financial dreams might seem daunting, but fear not! We've got the tips and tricks to help you find that perfect balance. After all, what's the point of financial independence if it doesn't come with a side of joy and fulfillment?

Giving Back & Financial Impact:

Money can be a force for good, and this section is all about the heartwarming side of adulting – giving back. We'll explore how to incorporate charitable giving into your financial journey, supporting causes you care about without breaking the bank.

From micro-donations to volunteer work, we'll discuss the various ways you can make a positive impact on the world while still staying true to your financial goals. Because adulting isn't just about building personal wealth; it's about creating a positive ripple effect in the lives of others.

So, my fellow adventurers in adulting, grab

your metaphorical capes, and let's master

the art of financial independence together!

Because you're not just adulting; you're

conquering the world, one financial

milestone at a time.

Chapter 6: "Beyond Budgets: Building Wealth and Crafting Your Financial Legacy"

Hey, financial trailblazers! Welcome to the third and exciting chapter of your financial journey – where we're moving beyond the basics and diving into the realm of building wealth and creating a legacy. It's like leveling up in a video game, unlocking new skills, and discovering hidden treasures. Are you ready for the next adventure?

1. Investment Adventures:

Alright, let's talk investments – the secret sauce for building wealth. Investing might sound like a word reserved for Wall Street wizards, but fear not! We'll break down the fundamentals, explore different investment vehicles, and unveil the mysteries of the stock market.

Discover the magic of compound growth,

learn the art of diversification, and understand that investing isn't just for the rich; it's for everyone with a financial dream. So, grab your adventurer's hat, and let's embark on the thrilling journey of building wealth through strategic investments.

2. Real Estate Exploration:

Ever dreamt of owning your piece of the world? Real estate could be your golden ticket. In this section, we'll explore the world of property ownership – from the pros and cons of homeownership to the potential wealth-building opportunities in real estate investing.

Learn about mortgages, equity, and how to make informed decisions when stepping into the real estate arena. Whether you're dreaming of your first home or considering real estate as an investment strategy, we'll equip you with the knowledge to navigate the market confidently.

3. Entrepreneurial Ventures:

Ready to be your boss? Entrepreneurship is like a rollercoaster of risks, rewards, and resilience. In this section, we'll discuss the ins and outs of starting your own business, from crafting a business plan to navigating the challenges of entrepreneurship.

Discover the thrill of turning your passion into profit, learn about different business structures, and understand the financial aspects of running a successful venture. Because in the world of building wealth, entrepreneurship is your golden ticket to unlimited possibilities.

4. Mastering Financial Risks:

Risk-taking isn't just reserved for extreme sports; it's a crucial aspect of building wealth. We'll explore the concept of risk in the financial realm – from understanding your risk tolerance to making calculated decisions that align with your financial goals.

Learn about insurance as a risk management tool, explore the world of investment risks, and understand why taking strategic financial risks can be the key to unlocking new opportunities. Building wealth isn't about playing it safe all the time; it's about navigating risks with wisdom and intention.

5. Crafting Your Financial Legacy:

Beyond building wealth lies the profound concept of crafting a legacy. What impact do you want to leave on the world? In this section, we'll explore the power of generational wealth, estate planning, and the role of philanthropy in shaping your financial legacy.

Learn about wills, trusts, and how to pass on not just financial assets but also the values and principles that define your family's legacy. Discover the joy of giving back and understand how your financial decisions today can create a lasting impact for generations to come.

6. The Road Ahead: Financial Mastery:

As we conclude this chapter, remember that building wealth and crafting a legacy is an ongoing journey. It's not about reaching a destination but about continually evolving, learning, and adapting to the ever-changing financial landscape.

Explore the possibilities, embrace the challenges, and stay curious about the vast opportunities that the world of finance offers. Your financial mastery is a lifelong adventure, and with the knowledge gained in this chapter, you're well-equipped to navigate the twists and turns that lie ahead.

So, my fellow financial adventurers, let's continue this exciting journey of building wealth, creating legacies, and mastering the art of financial success. The road ahead is filled with opportunities waiting to be discovered, and you're ready to conquer it all!

Conclusion:

As we draw the curtains on this exploration of "Golden Years and Beyond: Embracing Retirement and Legacy," it's not just about numbers and investments; it's about the heart and soul of your life's narrative.

Reflecting on the Journey: Your retirement isn't just a destination; it's a journey, a transition to a new chapter filled with opportunities for self-discovery, adventure, and purpose. Take a moment to reflect on the milestones you've passed, the challenges you've overcome, and the triumphs that have shaped you.

The Symphony of Legacy: Crafting a legacy is akin to composing a symphony. It involves not just financial instruments but the delicate harmonies of family values, shared memories, and the impact you leave on the world. Consider the resonance you wish to create in the lives of those you love and the broader community.

Beyond Finances:

While we've delved into financial strategies and investment wisdom, remember that retirement is a canvas waiting for the strokes of your passions. Embrace new horizons, explore uncharted territories, and find joy in the pursuits that fuel your soul. Family Bonds: The conversations about your legacy aren't merely about assets and distributions; they are about weaving stronger family bonds. Approach these discussions with openness, share your values, and foster understanding among generations. Your legacy is a tapestry, and each family member contributes to its vibrant hues.

The Gift of Time:

As you step into retirement, time becomes

your most precious asset. Use it wisely,

savoring the moments with loved ones,

pursuing dreams set aside, and immersing

yourself in the simple joys that make life

truly rich.

Health as Wealth:

The true wealth of retirement lies not just in

financial security but in your health and

well-being. Navigate the healthcare

landscape with diligence, prioritize self-care,

and embrace the opportunities for wellness

that this stage of life brings.

Gratitude and Giving:

Lastly, gratitude and giving back add depth and meaning to your legacy. Whether through charitable endeavors or small acts of kindness, the impact you make on others creates ripples that extend far beyond your own journey.

As you embark on this chapter of "Golden Years and Beyond," remember that retirement is not the end of a story; it's the beginning of a new narrative—one that you have the power to shape and fill with purpose. May your retirement be a canvas painted with joy, love, and the profound satisfaction of a life well-lived.

Here's to embracing the golden years

with open hearts and creating a legacy

that resonates for generations to come.

Cheers to your journey of fulfillment and

lasting impact!

Here are ten different business plan ideas tailored for singles, couples, families just starting on their own, and those starting over after a divorce:

1. Singles: Personal Development Coaching

Business Idea: A personal development coaching service focused on helping singles improve various aspects of their lives, including career advancement, financial management, self-care, and relationship building.

Key Components:

Target Market: Singles aged 25-40 who are seeking personal growth.

Services: One-on-one coaching sessions, group workshops, online courses, and motivational events.

Revenue Streams: Coaching fees, online course sales, membership subscriptions.

Marketing Strategy: Social media campaigns, collaborations with influencers, hosting free webinars to attract clients.

Expansion Opportunities: Launching a personal development app or writing a book on self-improvement.

2. Couples: Relationship Wellness Retreats

Business Idea: A boutique service offering wellness retreats designed to help couples strengthen their relationships through activities like yoga, meditation, couples counseling, and adventure sports.

Key Components:

Target Market: Couples aged 25-50 looking to enhance their relationship.

Services: Weekend retreats, wellness

workshops, relationship counseling, and follow-up online sessions.

Revenue Streams: Retreat fees, counseling sessions, merchandise sales (e.g., wellness products).

Marketing Strategy: Partnering with travel agencies, social media marketing, offering early-bird discounts.

Expansion Opportunities: Offering retreats internationally, creating an online community for couples.

3. Families Just Starting: Home Organization and Decluttering Service

Business Idea: A professional home

organization service that helps new families create functional and beautiful living spaces by organizing and decluttering their homes.

Key Components:

Target Market: Young families or couples who have just bought their first home.

Services: In-home organization, decluttering consultations, storage solutions, and moving assistance.

Revenue Streams: Service fees, sales of organization products, online workshops.

Marketing Strategy: Local advertising, word-of-mouth referrals, partnerships with real estate agents.

Expansion Opportunities: Launching a YouTube channel with home organization tips, writing a blog.

4. Singles: Solo Travel Planning Service

Business Idea: A travel agency specializing in planning and organizing trips for solo travelers, focusing on safety, cultural experiences, and social opportunities.

Key Components:

Target Market: Singles aged 20-45 who enjoy traveling alone.

Services: Customized travel itineraries, group travel for solo travelers, safety briefings, and local guides.

Revenue Streams: Travel planning fees, commissions from travel partners, group travel bookings.

Marketing Strategy: Collaborations with travel bloggers, targeted ads on social media, offering travel tips on a blog.

Expansion Opportunities: Launching a travel blog or app, organizing international solo travel meetups.

5. Couples: Online Couples Cooking Classes

Business Idea: A virtual platform offering live and recorded cooking classes for couples to enjoy together, focusing on creating memorable date night experiences at home.

Key Components:

Target Market: Couples aged 25-50 looking for unique date night ideas.

Services: Live cooking classes, pre-recorded lessons, recipe kits, and private cooking sessions.

Revenue Streams: Class fees, subscription plans, sales of recipe kits, and branded merchandise.

Marketing Strategy: Influencer partnerships, social media ads, email marketing with cooking tips.

Expansion Opportunities: Creating a cookbook, hosting in-person cooking events, launching a cooking show.

6. Families Just Starting: Family Financial Planning Service

Business Idea: A financial planning service tailored to help young families manage their finances, save for the future, and make smart investment decisions.

Key Components:

Target Market: New families and couples planning for children.

Services: Budget planning, investment advice, debt management, and college savings plans.

Revenue Streams: Consultation fees, financial planning packages, and commissions from financial products.

Marketing Strategy: Partnering with real estate agents, offering free financial webinars, referral programs.

Expansion Opportunities: Developing a financial planning app, publishing a family finance guidebook.

7. Singles: Fitness and Wellness Subscription Box

Business Idea: A subscription box service that delivers fitness and wellness products to singles focused on maintaining a healthy lifestyle.

Key Components:

Target Market: Health-conscious singles aged 20-40.

Products: Fitness gear, healthy snacks,

wellness supplements, and workout plans.

Revenue Streams: Subscription fees, sales of individual products, affiliate marketing.

Marketing Strategy: Social media influencer partnerships, unboxing videos, email marketing.

Expansion Opportunities: Launching a fitness app, offering personalized wellness coaching.

8. Couples: Couples Counseling and Wellness App

Business Idea: An app that offers couples counseling, relationship advice, and wellness resources to help couples

maintain a healthy and happy

relationship.

Key Components:

Target Market: Couples aged 25-50

looking for relationship support.

Services: Virtual counseling sessions,

relationship quizzes, guided meditation,

and wellness tips.

Revenue Streams: App subscription

fees, in-app purchases, affiliate

marketing.

Marketing Strategy: Social media ads,

partnerships with relationship influencers, free trial offers.

Expansion Opportunities: Offering in-person counseling sessions, launching a relationship podcast.

9. Families Just Starting: Family-Friendly Meal Delivery Service

Business Idea: A meal delivery service that provides healthy, family-friendly meals designed to make dinnertime easier for busy families.

Key Components:

Target Market: New parents and young

families.

Products: Pre-prepared meals, meal kits, healthy snacks, and special occasion catering.

Revenue Streams: Subscription fees, one-time meal orders, catering services.

Marketing Strategy: Local advertising, partnerships with parenting bloggers, offering discounts for new subscribers.

Expansion Opportunities: Expanding to new cities, offering cooking classes for families.

10. Divorced Individuals: Life Reboot Coaching Service

Business Idea: A coaching service designed to help individuals navigate life after divorce, focusing on rebuilding confidence, career coaching, and personal development.

Key Components:

Target Market: Recently divorced individuals aged 30-50.

Services: One-on-one coaching, group workshops, career counseling, and personal development courses.

Revenue Streams: Coaching fees, online course sales, group workshop fees.

Marketing Strategy: Social media campaigns, partnerships with divorce lawyers, hosting free webinars.

Expansion Opportunities: Writing a book on life after divorce, launching a support community or app.

Here are ten different business plan ideas tailored for singles, couples, families just starting on their own, and those starting over after a divorce:

1. Singles: Personal Development Coaching

Business Idea: A personal development coaching service focused on helping singles improve various aspects of their lives, including career advancement, financial management, self-care, and

relationship building.

Key Components:

Target Market: Singles aged 25-40 who

are seeking personal growth.

Services: One-on-one coaching

sessions, group workshops, online

courses, and motivational events.

Revenue Streams: Coaching fees,

online course sales, membership

subscriptions.

Marketing Strategy: Social media

campaigns, collaborations with

influencers, hosting free webinars to

attract clients.

Expansion Opportunities: Launching a

personal development app or writing a

book on self-improvement.

2. Couples: Relationship Wellness Retreats

Business Idea: A boutique service offering wellness retreats designed to help couples strengthen their relationships through activities like yoga, meditation, couples counseling, and adventure sports.

Key Components:

Target Market: Couples aged 25-50 looking to enhance their relationship.

Services: Weekend retreats, wellness workshops, relationship counseling, and follow-up online sessions.

Revenue Streams: Retreat fees, counseling sessions, merchandise sales (e.g., wellness products).

Marketing Strategy: Partnering with travel agencies, social media marketing, offering early-bird discounts.

Expansion Opportunities: Offering retreats internationally, creating an online community for couples.

3. Families Just Starting: Home Organization and Decluttering Service

Business Idea: A professional home organization service that helps new families create functional and beautiful living spaces by organizing and decluttering their homes.

Key Components:

Target Market: Young families or couples who have just bought their first home.

Services: In-home organization, decluttering consultations, storage solutions, and moving assistance.

Revenue Streams: Service fees, sales of organization products, online workshops.

Marketing Strategy: Local advertising, word-of-mouth referrals, partnerships with real estate agents.

Expansion Opportunities: Launching a YouTube channel with home organization tips, writing a blog.

4. Singles: Solo Travel Planning Service

Business Idea: A travel agency specializing in planning and organizing trips for solo travelers, focusing on safety, cultural experiences, and social opportunities.

Key Components:

Target Market: Singles aged 20-45 who enjoy traveling alone.

Services: Customized travel itineraries, group travel for solo travelers, safety briefings, and local guides.

Revenue Streams: Travel planning fees,

commissions from travel partners,

group travel bookings.

Marketing Strategy: Collaborations with

travel bloggers, targeted ads on social

media, offering travel tips on a blog.

Expansion Opportunities: Launching a

travel blog or app, organizing

international solo travel meetups.

5. Couples: Online Couples Cooking Classes

Business Idea: A virtual platform offering live and recorded cooking classes for couples to enjoy together, focusing on creating memorable date night experiences at home.

Key Components:

Target Market: Couples aged 25-50 looking for unique date night ideas.

Services: Live cooking classes, pre-recorded lessons, recipe kits, and private cooking sessions.

Revenue Streams: Class fees, subscription plans, sales of recipe kits, and branded merchandise.

Marketing Strategy: Influencer partnerships, social media ads, email marketing with cooking tips.

Expansion Opportunities: Creating a cookbook, hosting in-person cooking events, launching a cooking show.

6. Families Just Starting: Family Financial Planning Service

Business Idea: A financial planning service tailored to help young families manage their finances, save for the future, and make smart investment decisions.

Key Components:

Target Market: New families and couples planning for children.

Services: Budget planning, investment advice, debt management, and college savings plans.

Revenue Streams: Consultation fees, financial planning packages, and commissions from financial products.

Marketing Strategy: Partnering with real estate agents, offering free financial webinars, referral programs.

Expansion Opportunities: Developing a financial planning app, publishing a family finance guidebook.

7. Singles: Fitness and Wellness Subscription Box

Business Idea: A subscription box service that delivers fitness and wellness products to singles focused on maintaining a healthy lifestyle.

Key Components:

Target Market: Health-conscious singles aged 20-40.

Products: Fitness gear, healthy snacks, wellness supplements, and workout plans.

Revenue Streams: Subscription fees,

sales of individual products, affiliate

marketing.

Marketing Strategy: Social media

influencer partnerships, unboxing

videos, email marketing.

Expansion Opportunities: Launching a

fitness app, offering personalized

wellness coaching.

8. Couples: Couples Counseling and Wellness App

Business Idea: An app that offers couples counseling, relationship advice, and wellness resources to help couples maintain a healthy and happy relationship.

Key Components:

Target Market: Couples aged 25-50 looking for relationship support.

Services: Virtual counseling sessions, relationship quizzes, guided meditation, and wellness tips.

Revenue Streams: App subscription fees, in-app purchases, affiliate marketing.

Marketing Strategy: Social media ads, partnerships with relationship influencers, free trial offers.

Expansion Opportunities: Offering in-person counseling sessions, launching a relationship podcast.

9. Families Just Starting: Family-Friendly Meal Delivery Service

Business Idea: A meal delivery service that provides healthy, family-friendly meals designed to make dinnertime easier for busy families.

Key Components:

Target Market: New parents and young families.

Products: Pre-prepared meals, meal kits, healthy snacks, and special occasion catering.

Revenue Streams: Subscription fees,

one-time meal orders, catering
services.

Marketing Strategy: Local advertising,
partnerships with parenting bloggers,
offering discounts for new subscribers.

Expansion Opportunities: Expanding to
new cities, offering cooking classes for
families.

10. Divorced Individuals: Life Reboot Coaching Service

Business Idea: A coaching service designed to help individuals navigate life after divorce, focusing on rebuilding confidence, career coaching, and personal development.

Key Components:

Target Market: Recently divorced individuals aged 30-50.

Services: One-on-one coaching, group workshops, career counseling, and personal development courses.

Revenue Streams: Coaching fees, online course sales, group workshop fees.

Marketing Strategy: Social media campaigns, partnerships with divorce lawyers, hosting free webinars.

Expansion Opportunities: Writing a book on life after divorce, launching a support community or app.

www.ingramcontent.com/pod-product-compliance
Lightning Source LLC
Chambersburg PA
CBHW021453210526
45463CB00002B/760